Tortoise

Words to practise

tortoise soil

down

asleep

The tortoise is
asleep in its shell.

The tortoise is out of its shell.

The tortoise digs in the soil.

The tortoise digs a tunnel in the soil.

Oh no! Soil falls down in the tunnel.

The tortoise digs the soil out of the tunnel.

At last the tortoise is out of the tunnel.